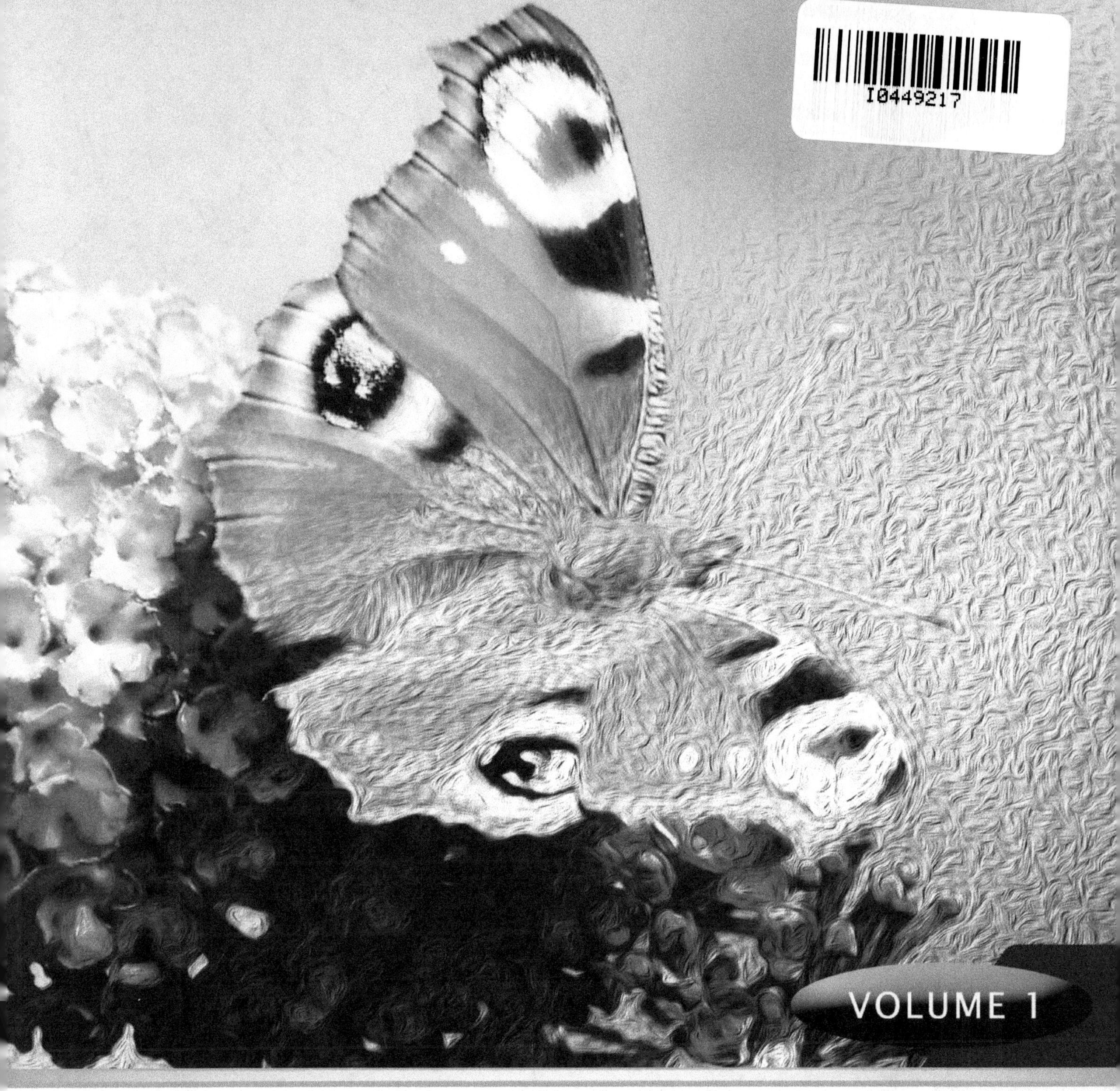

The Butterfly SHADING

A Grayscale Coloring Book

COLORING BOOK FOR ADULTS

COLOR TEST PAGE

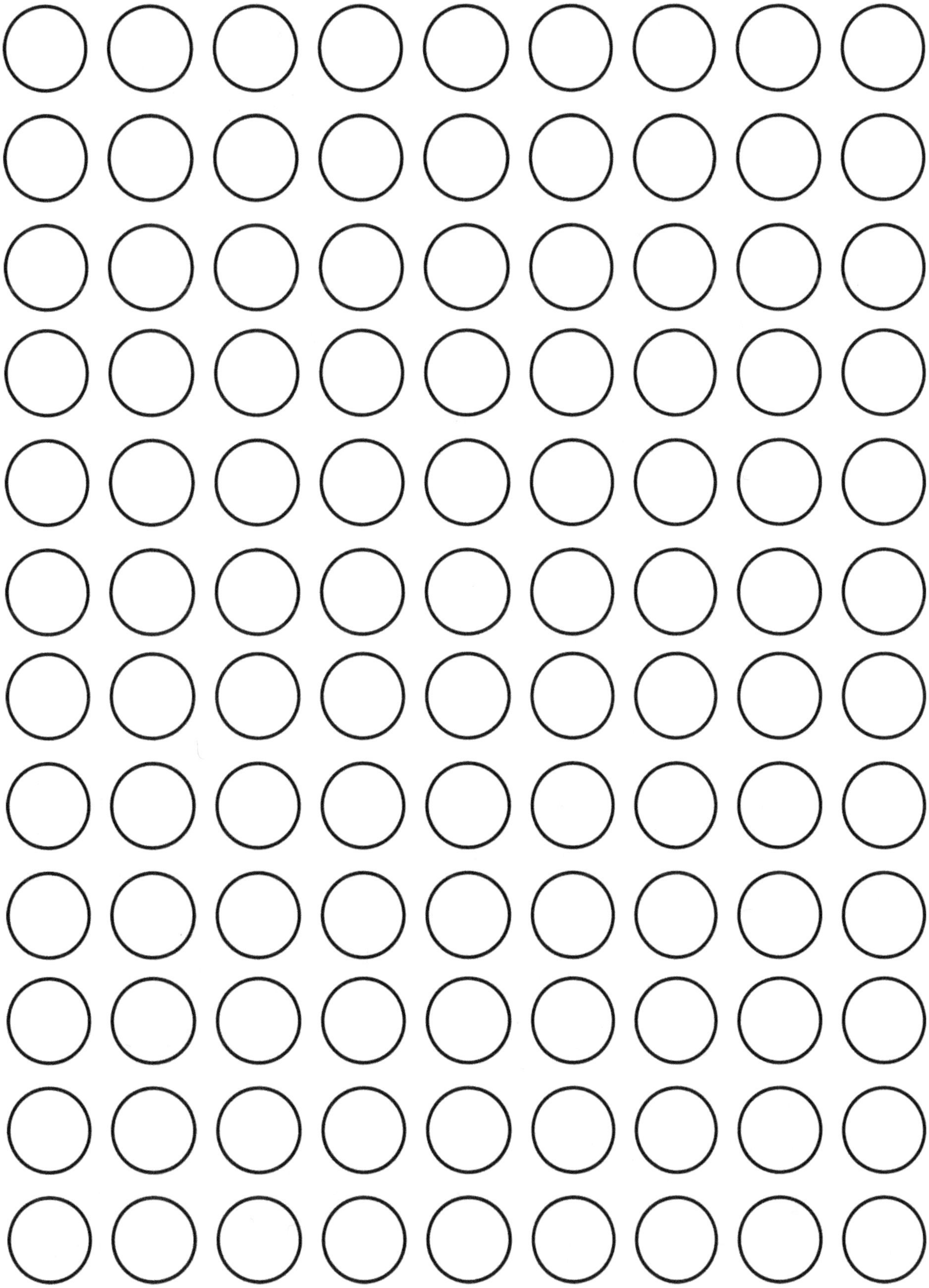

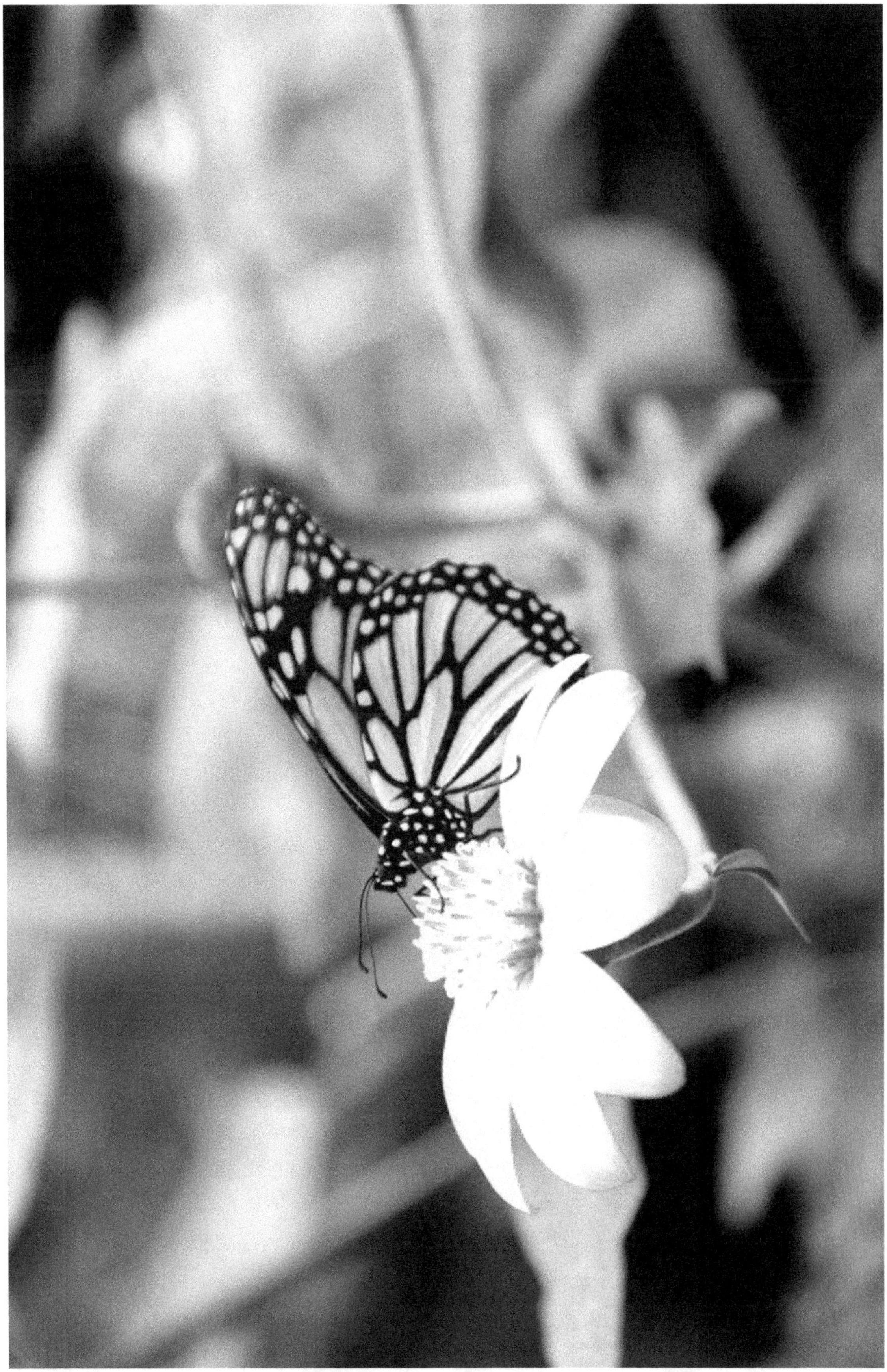

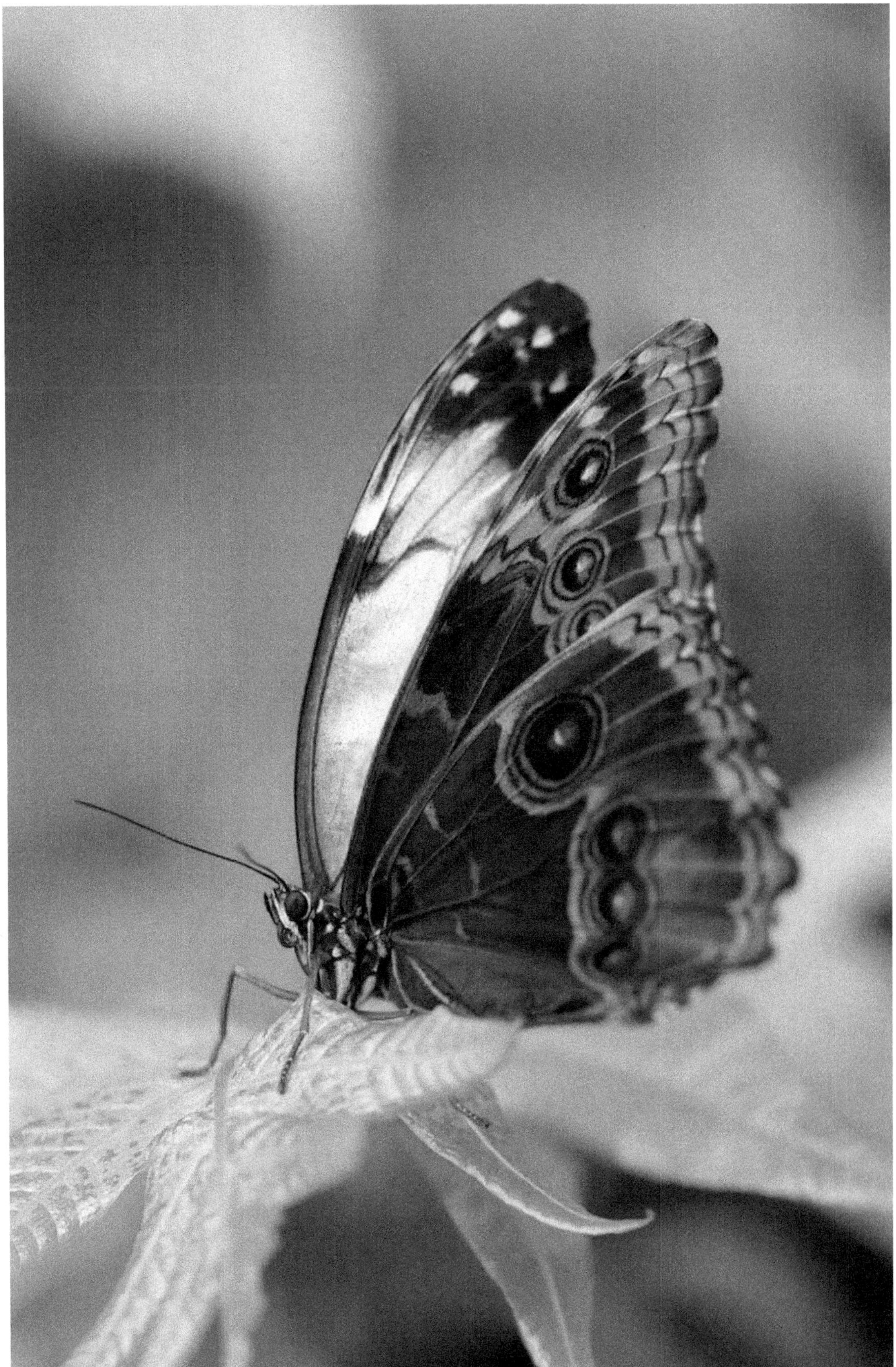

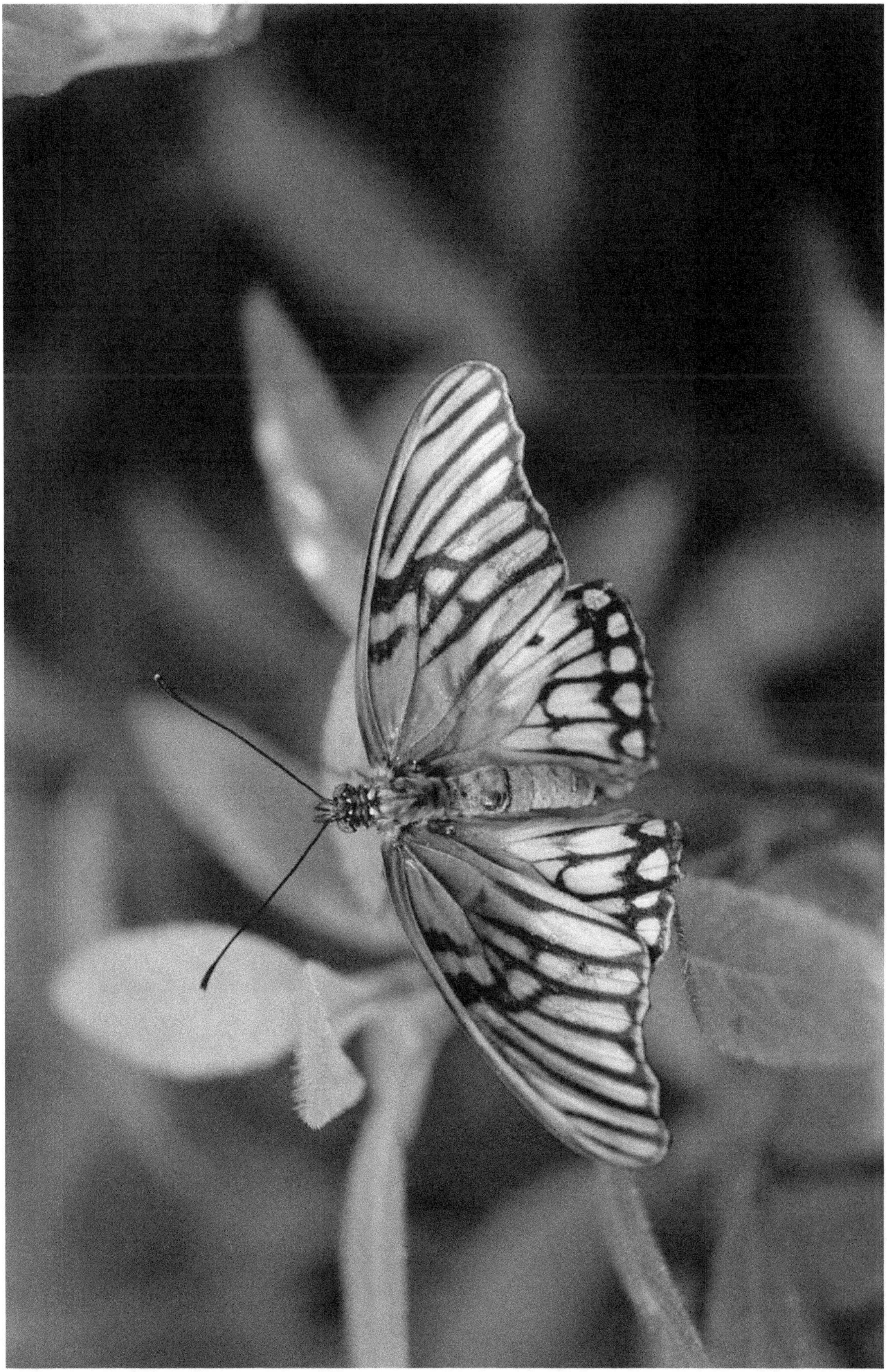

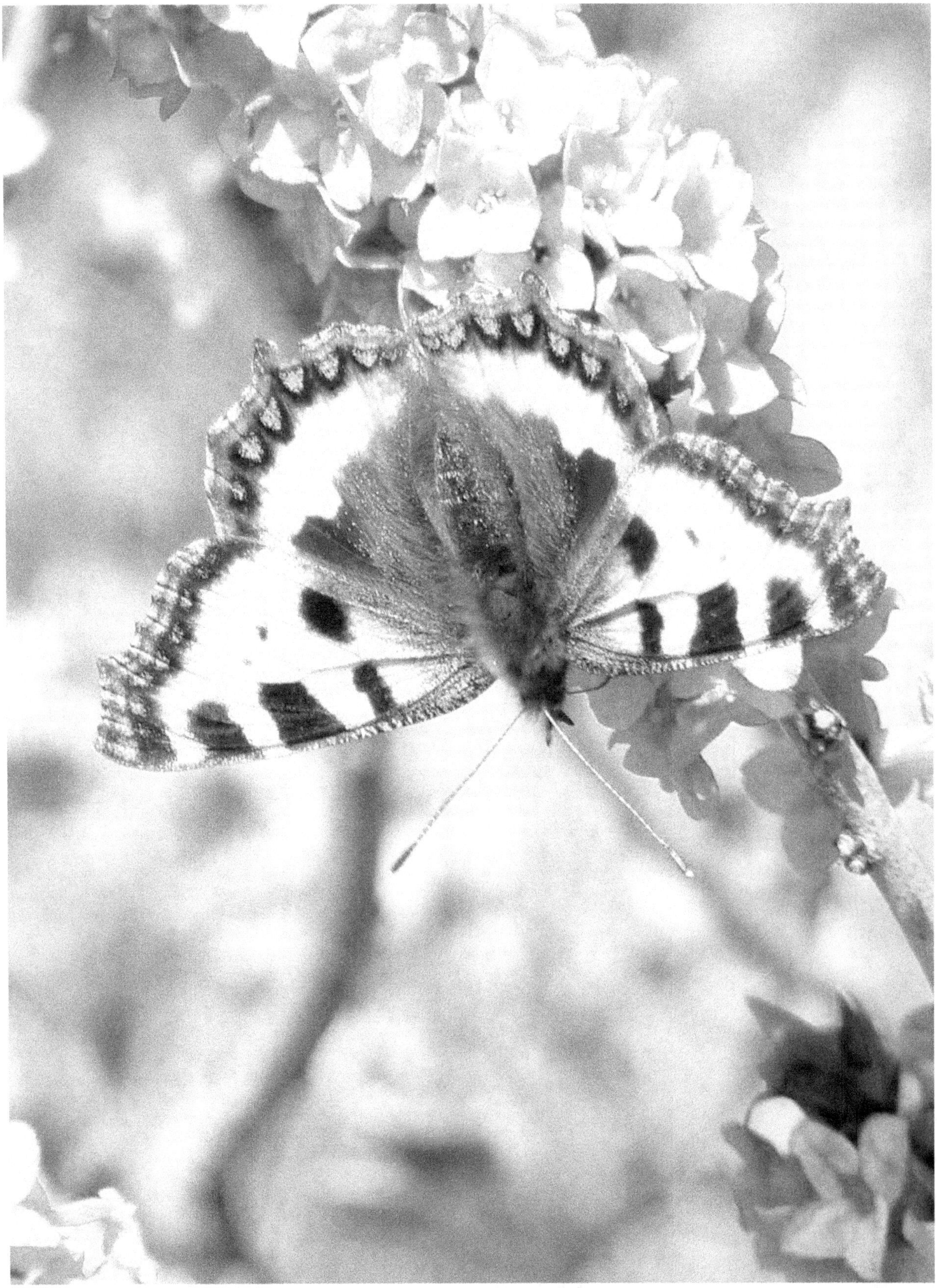

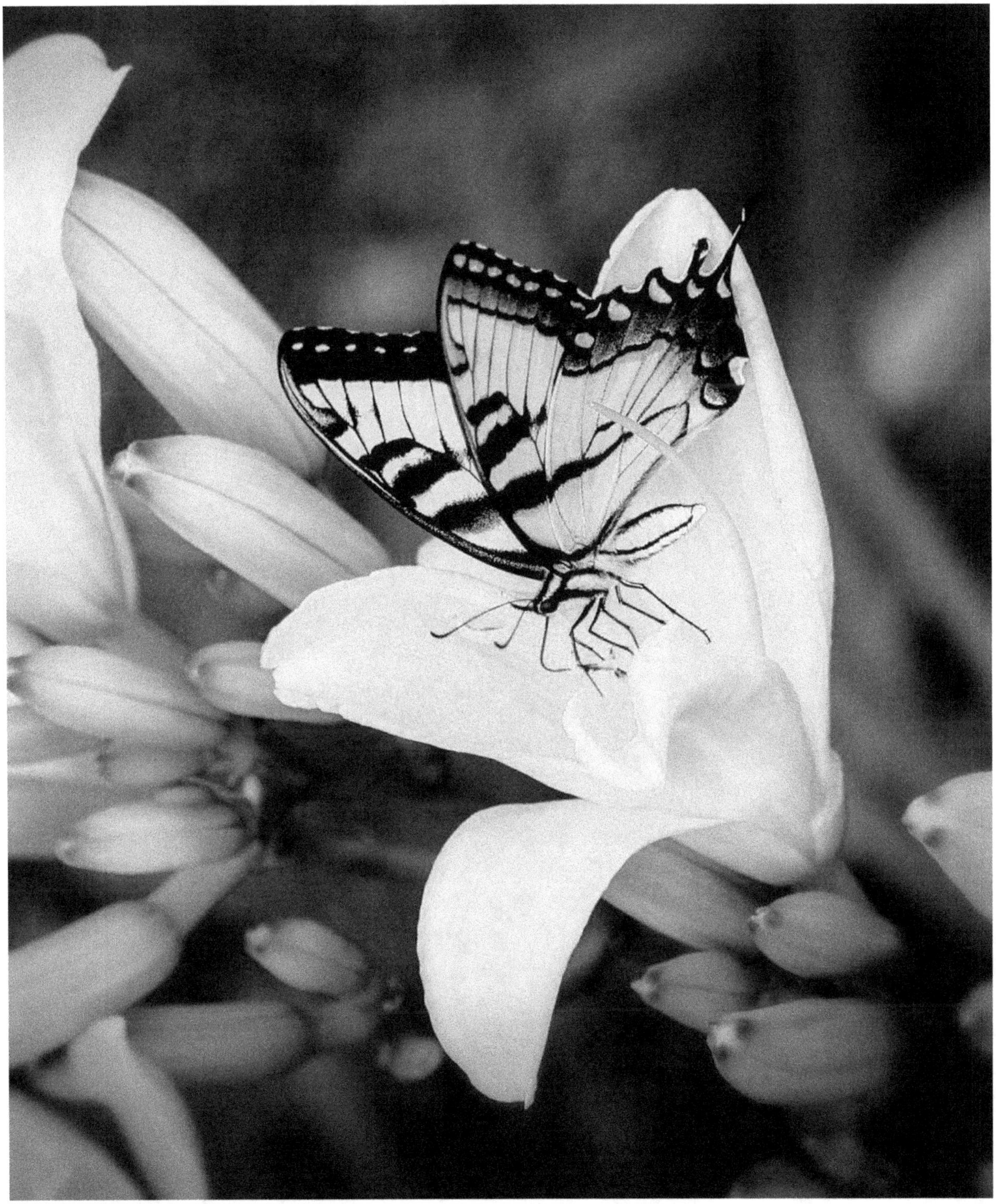

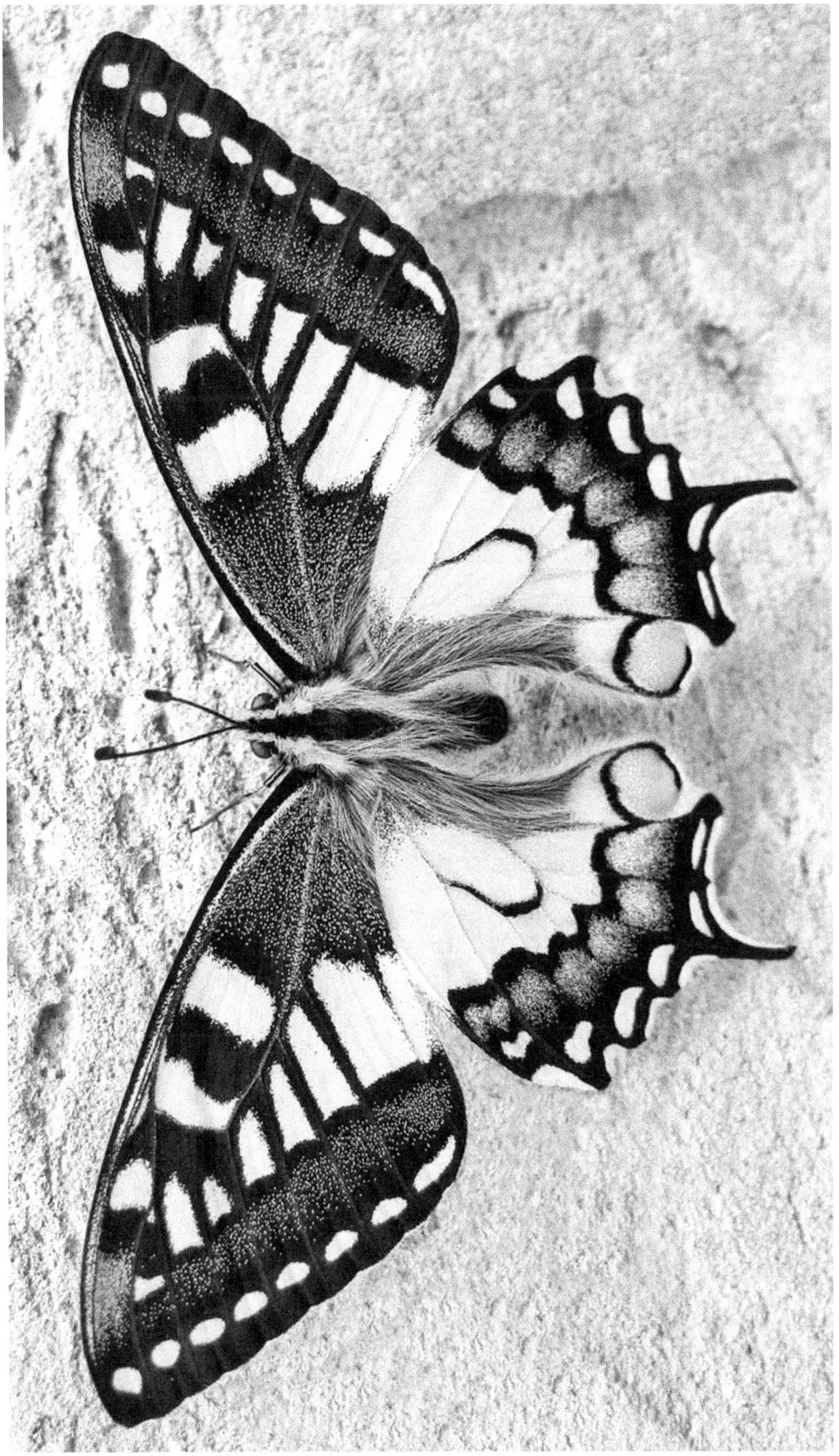

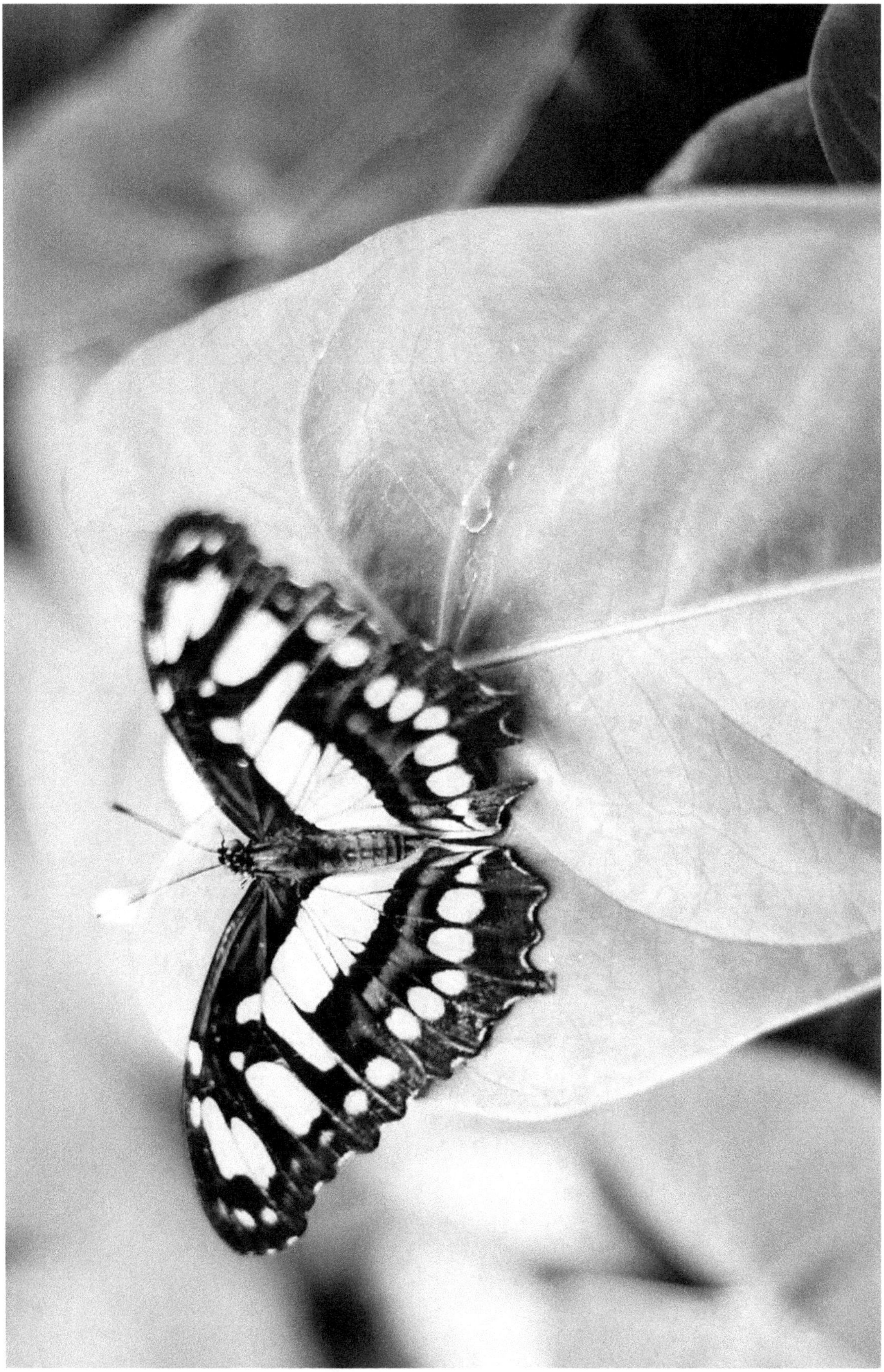

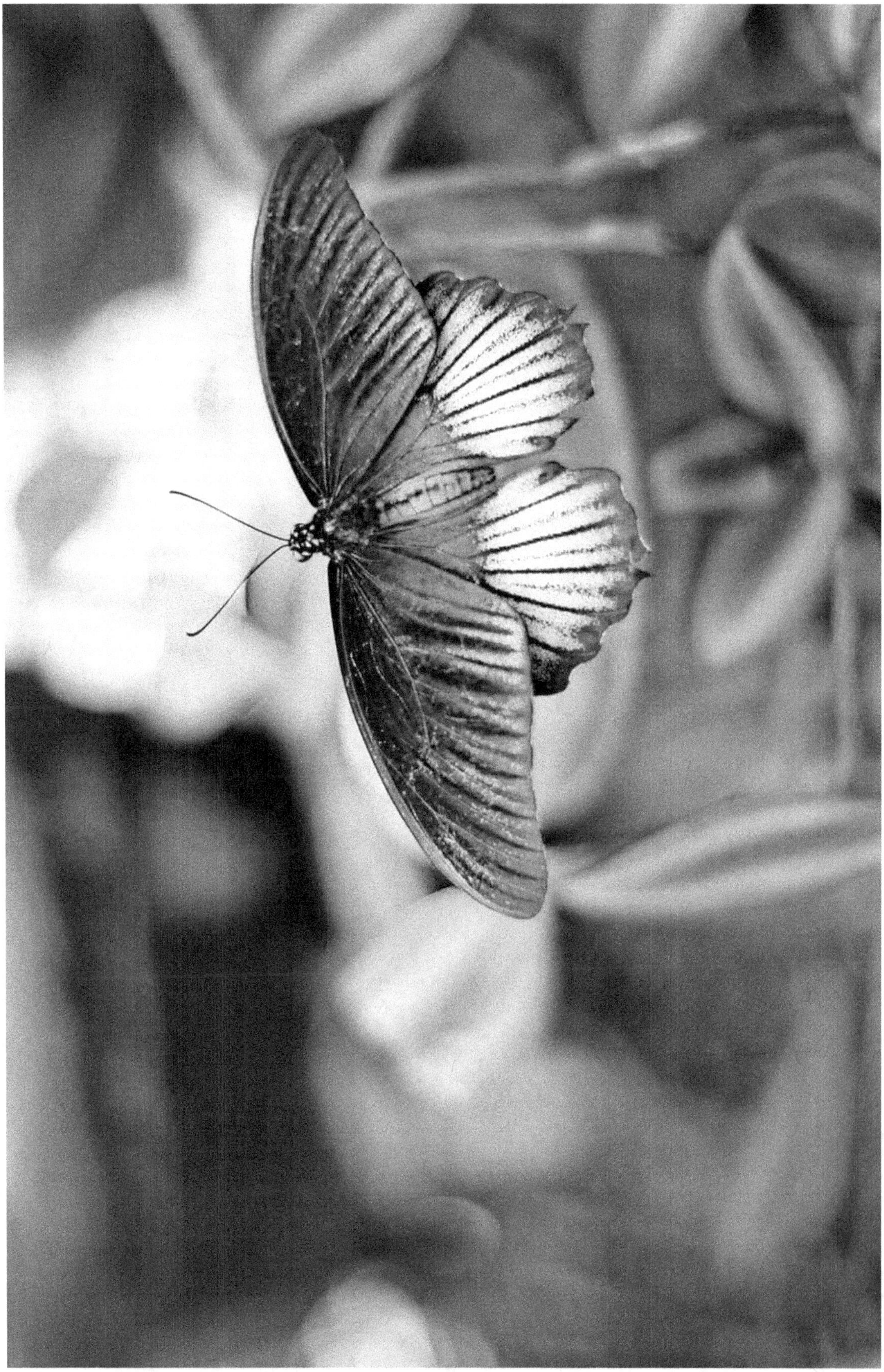

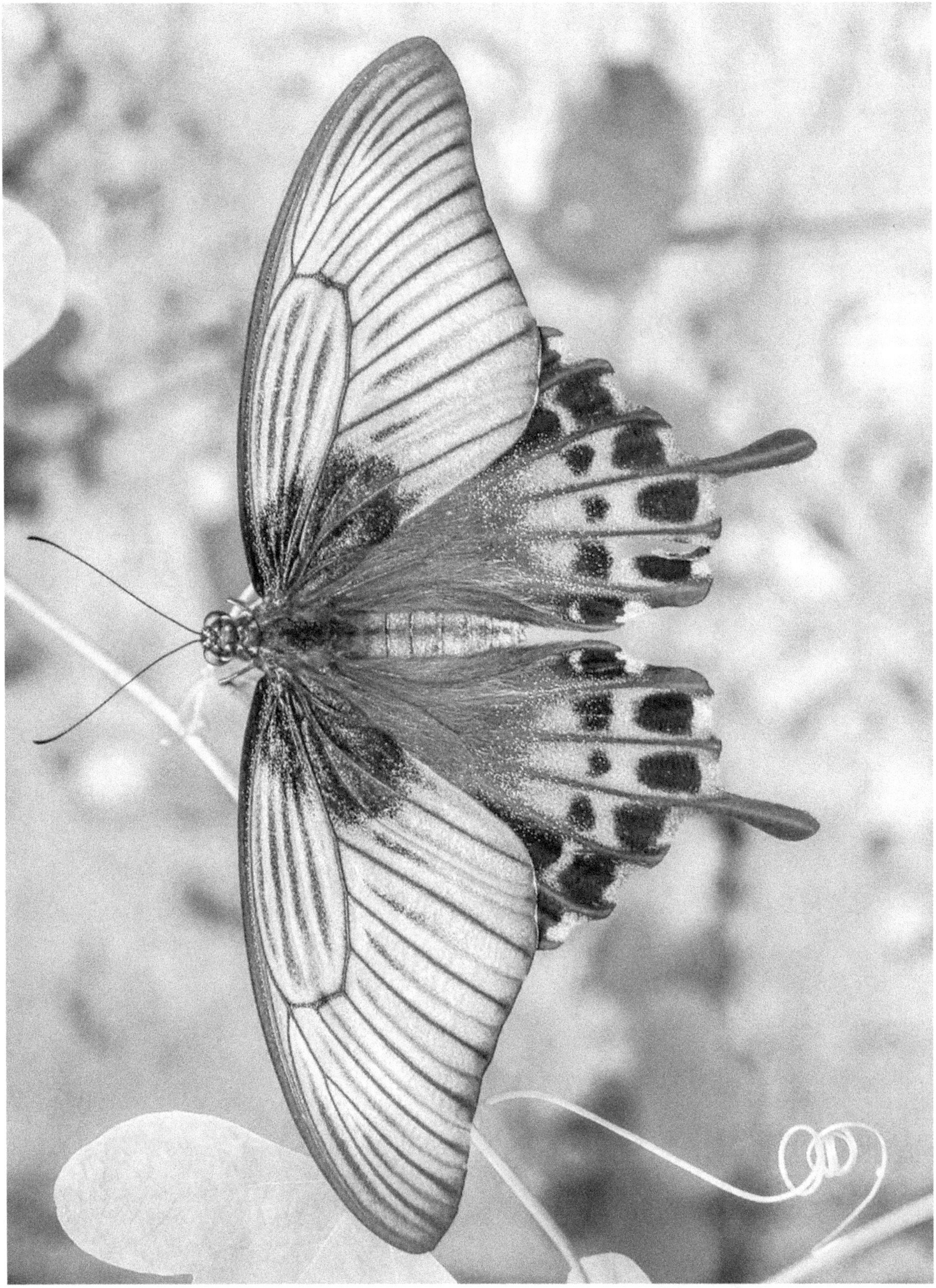

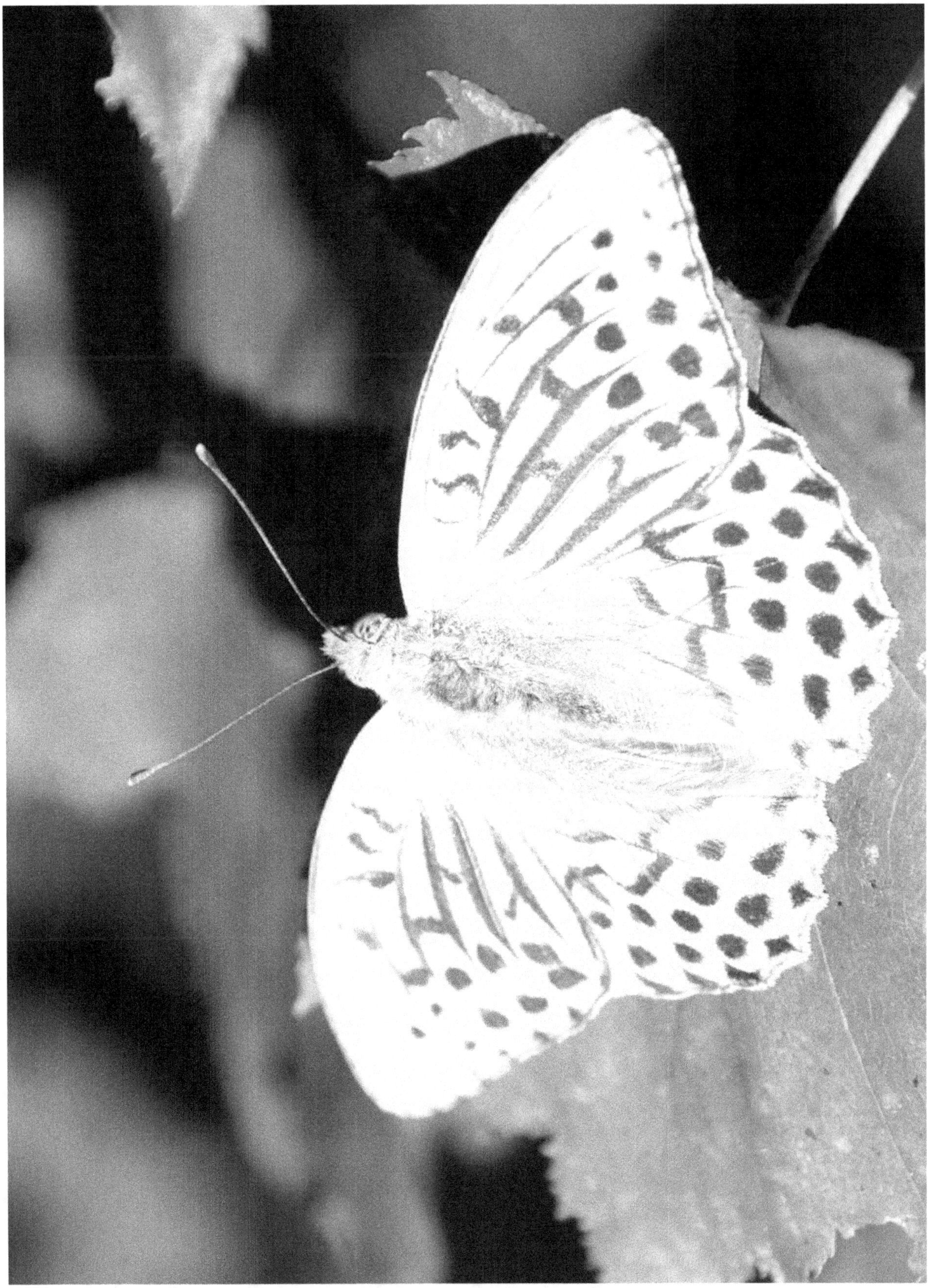

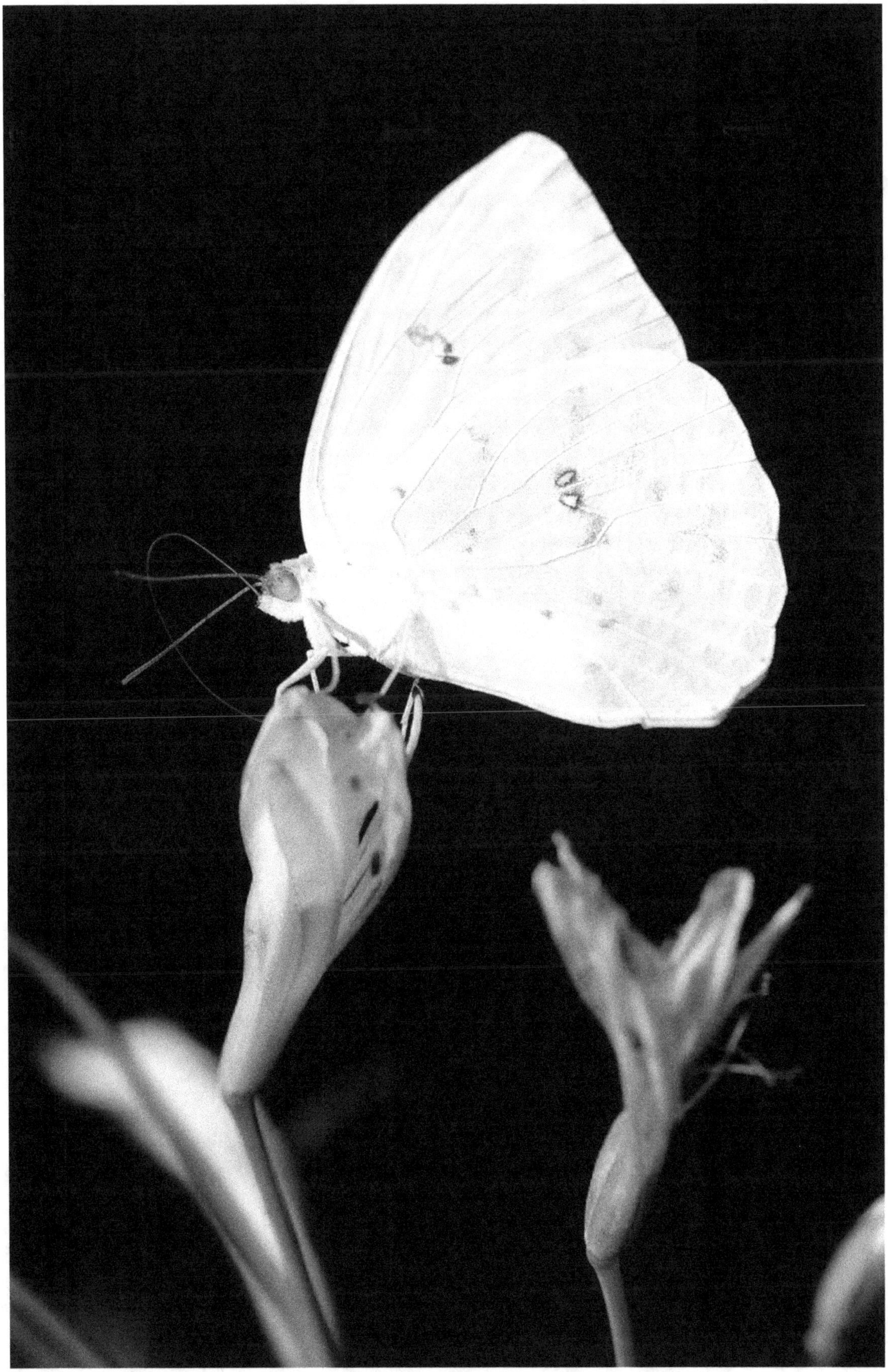

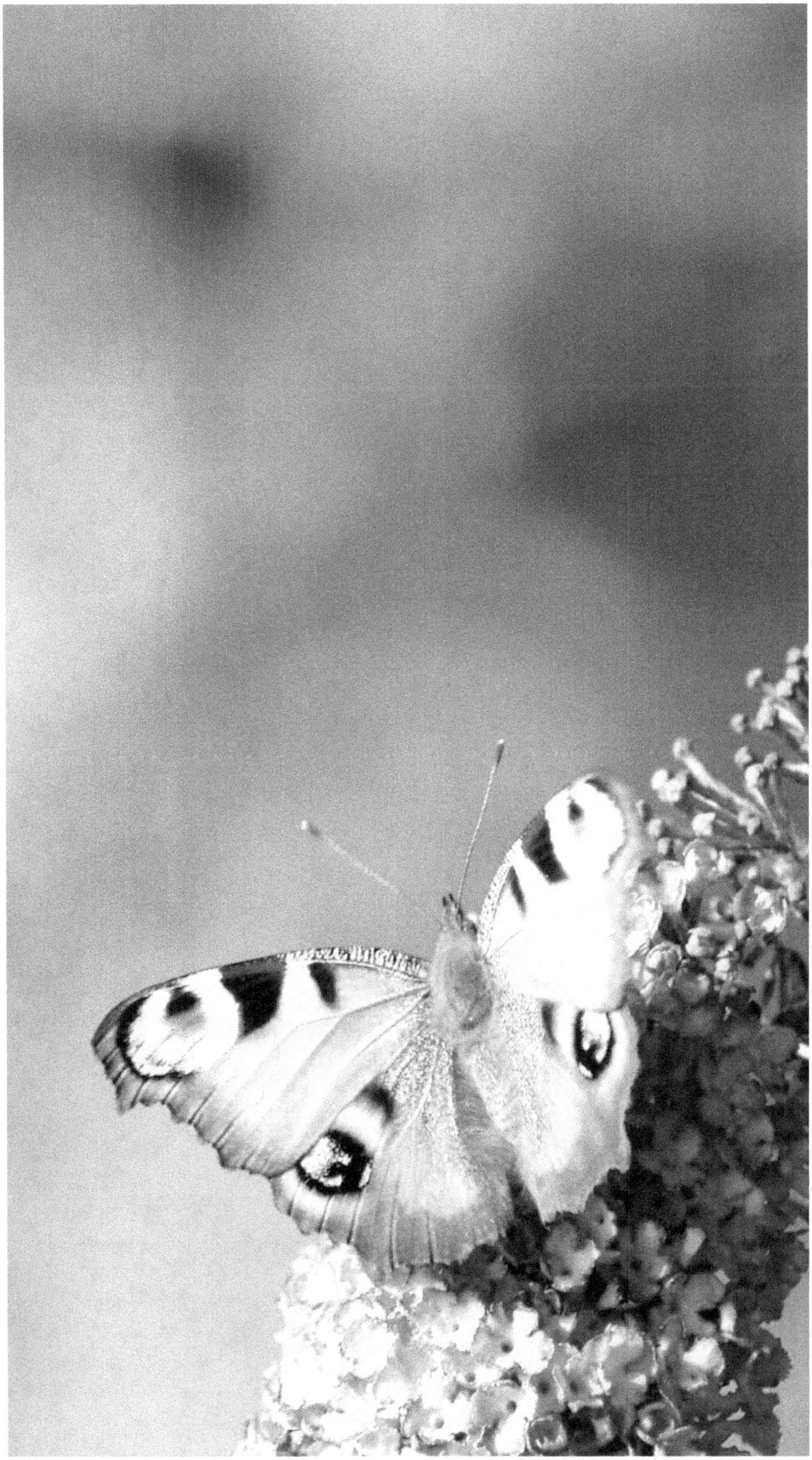

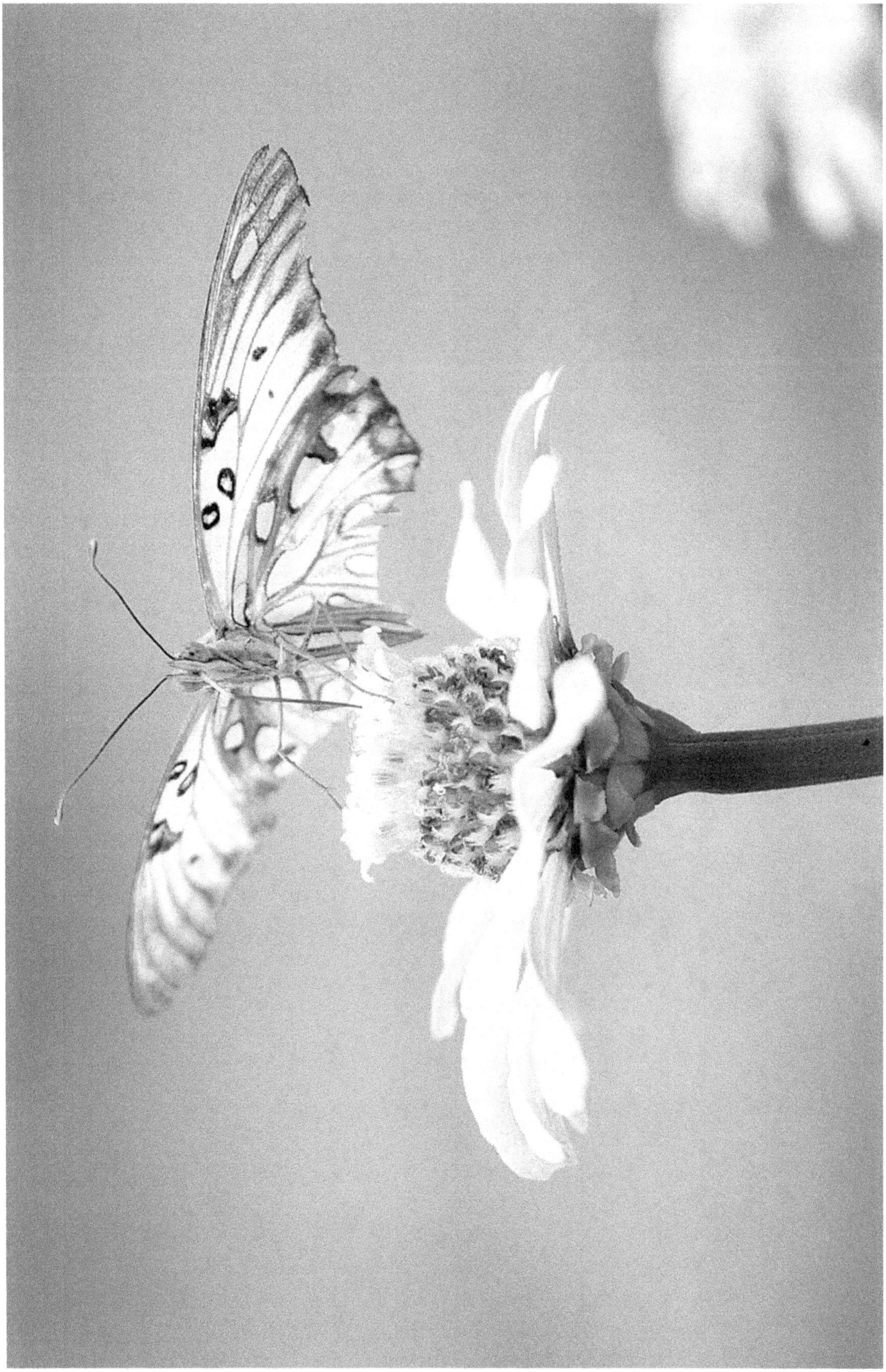

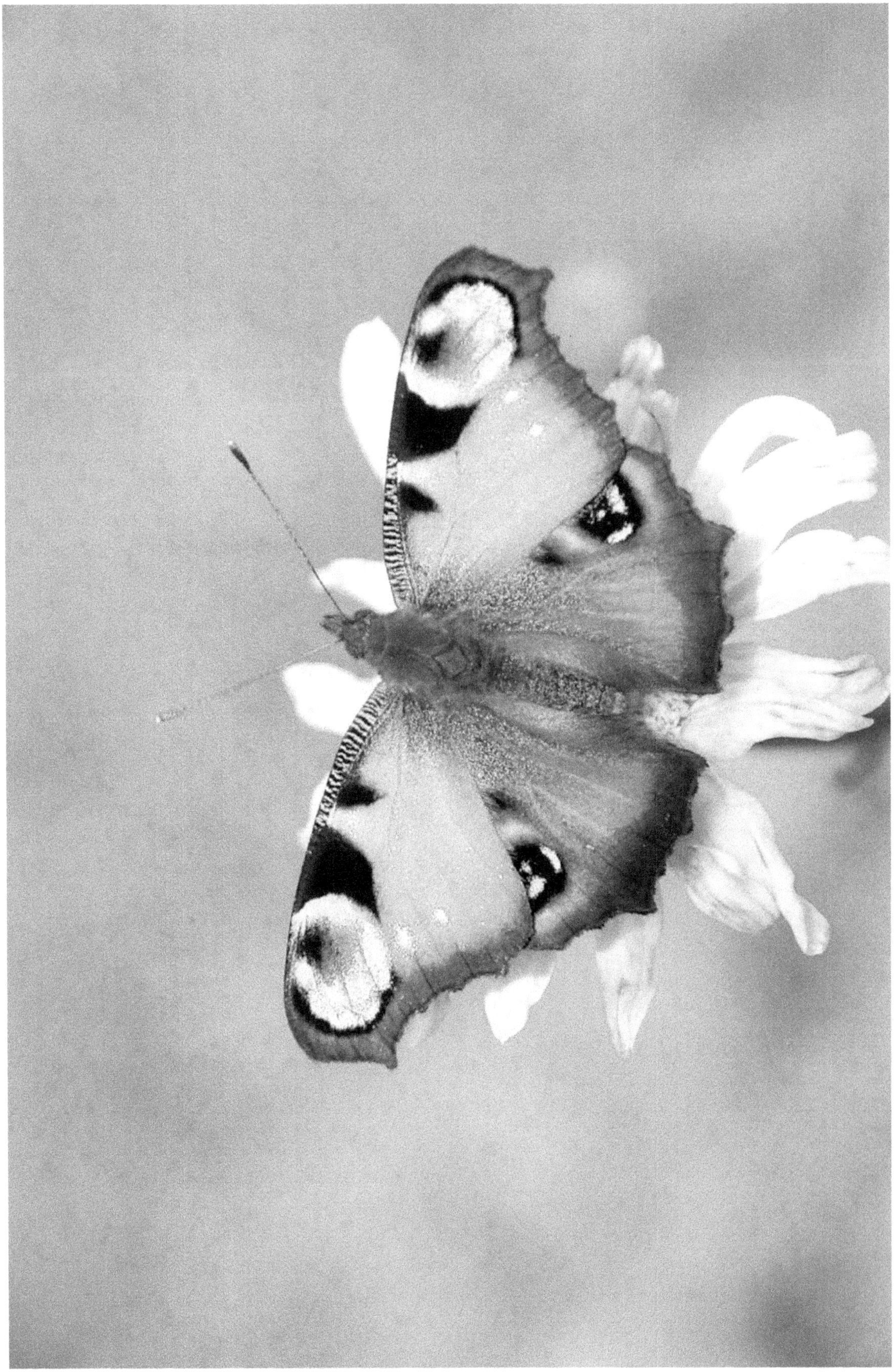

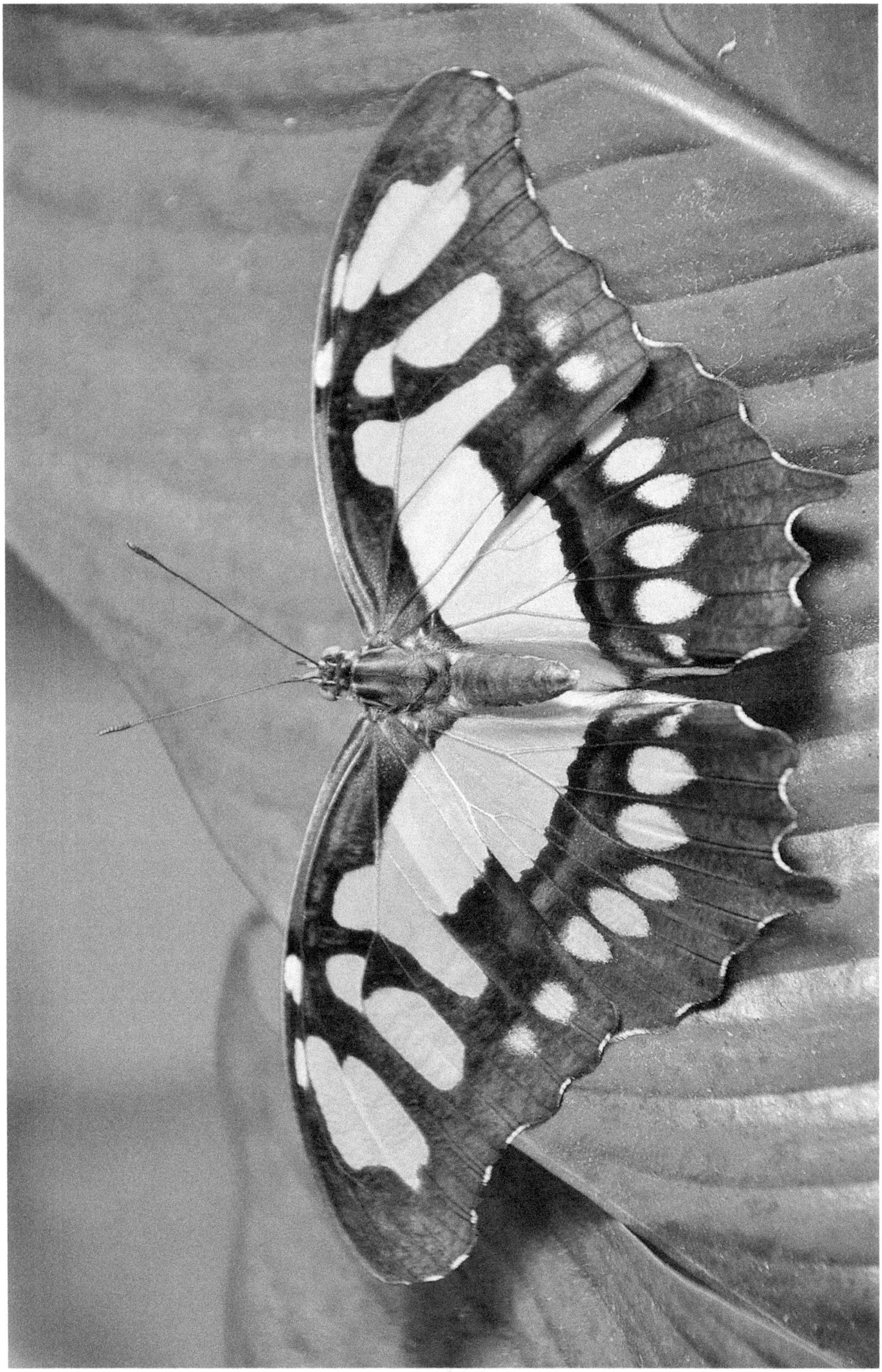

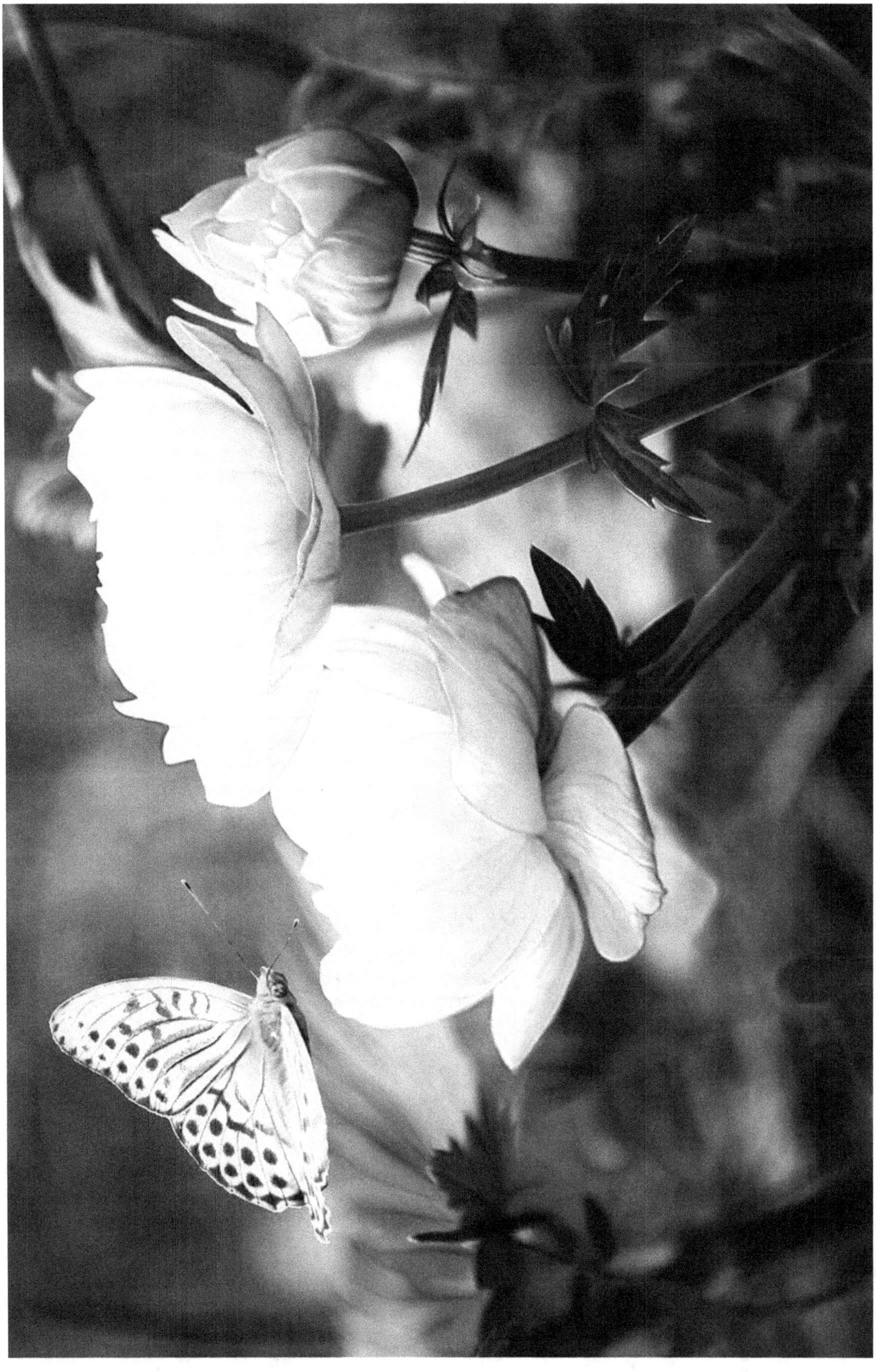

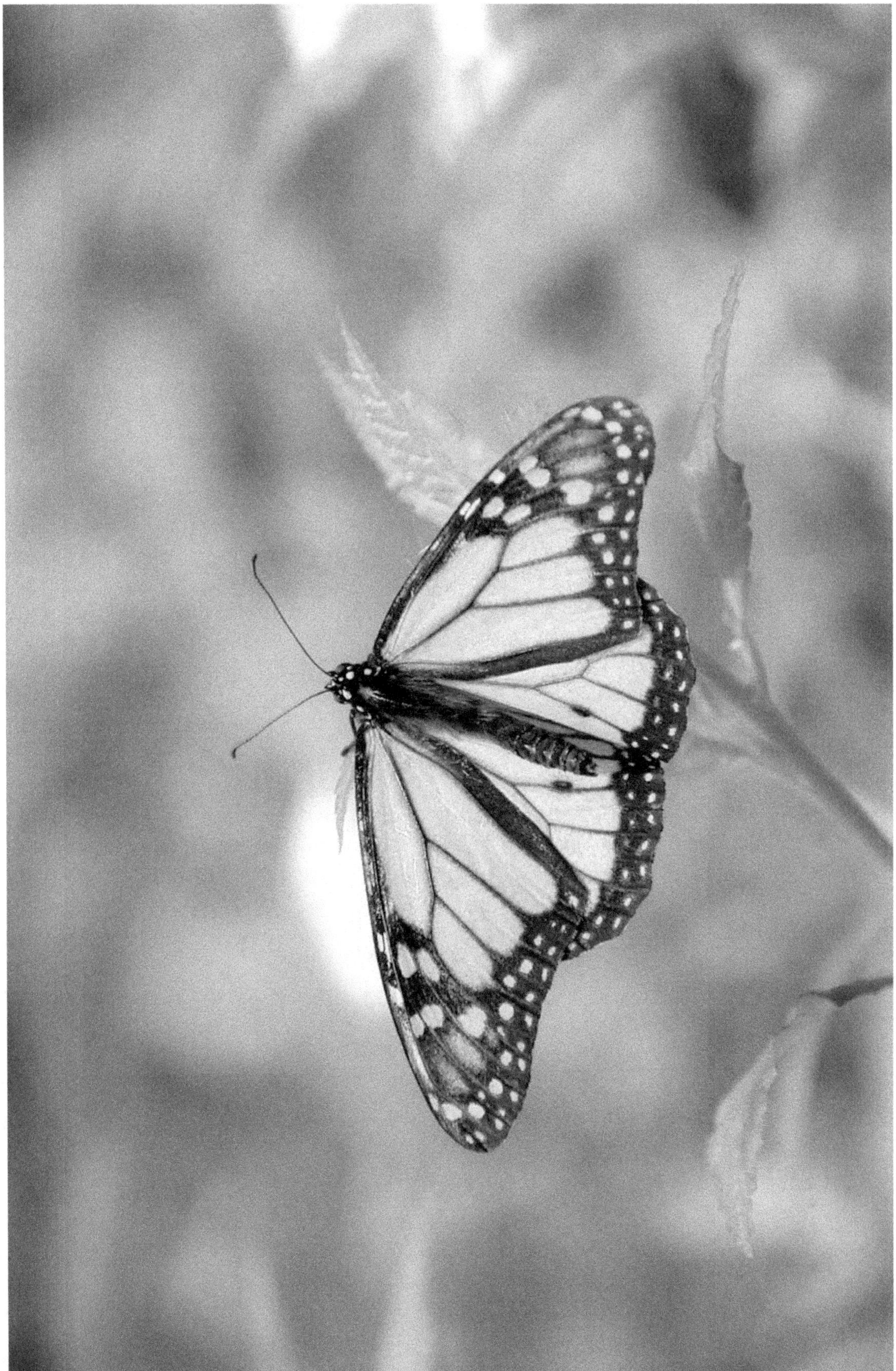

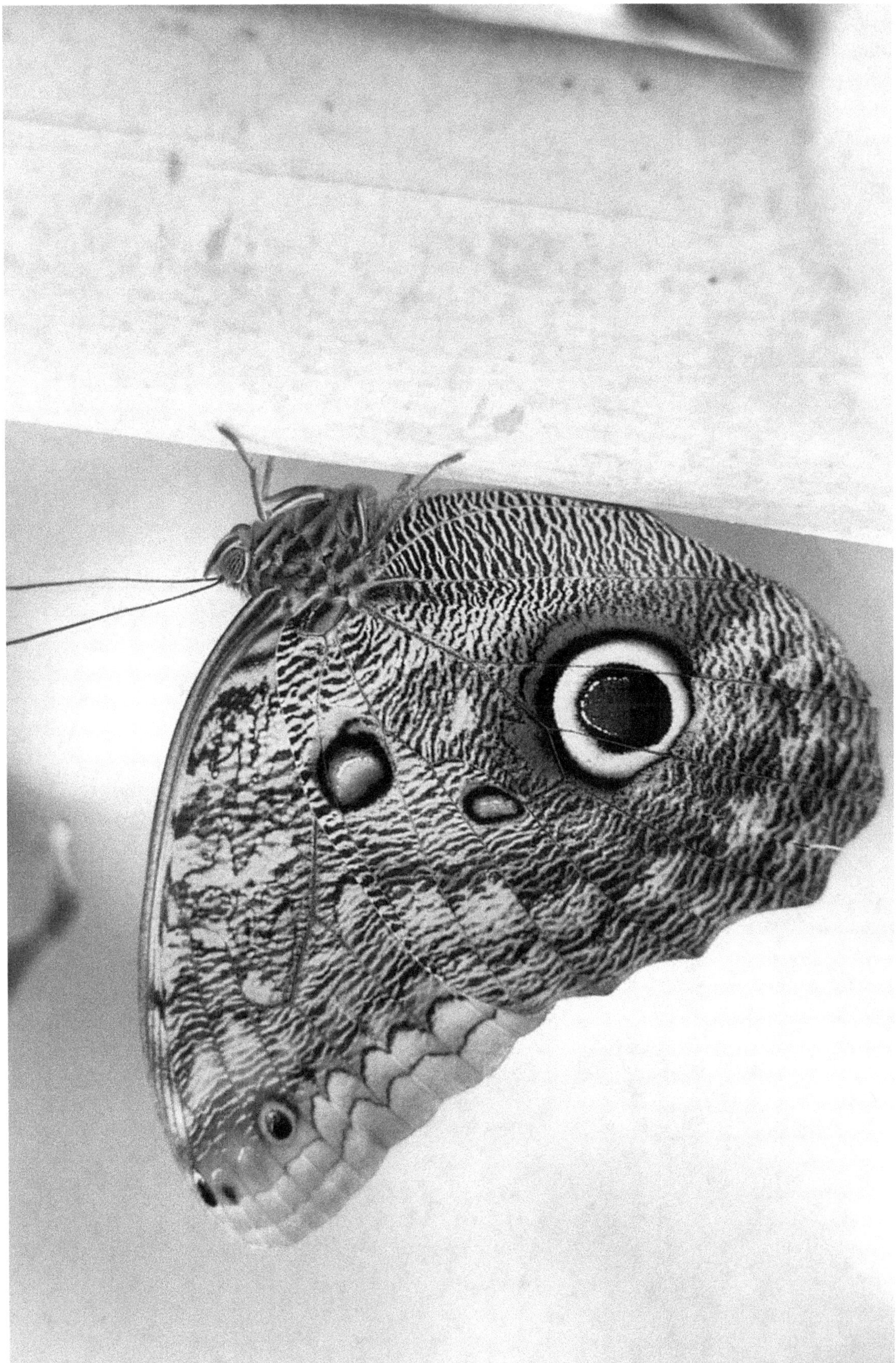

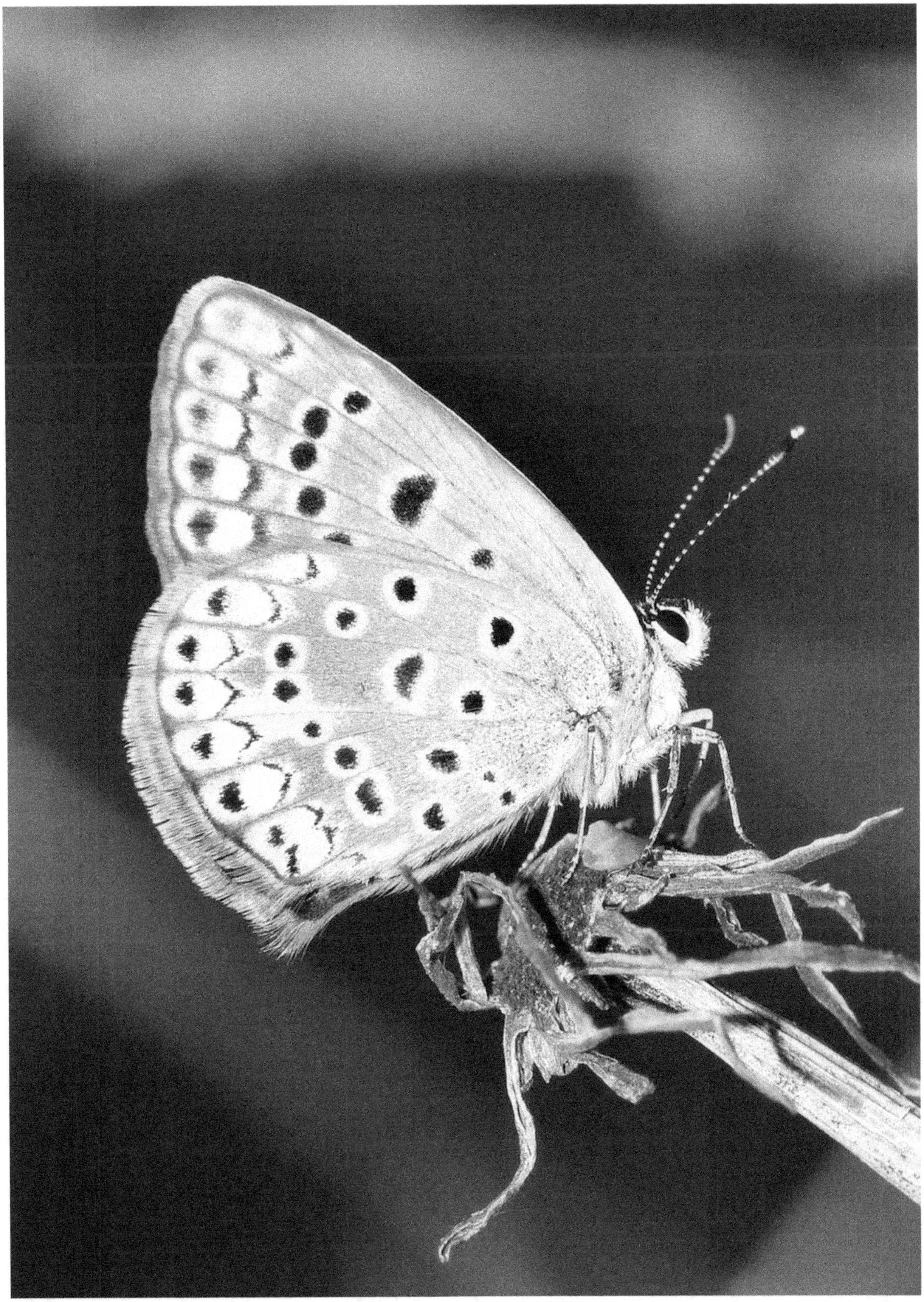

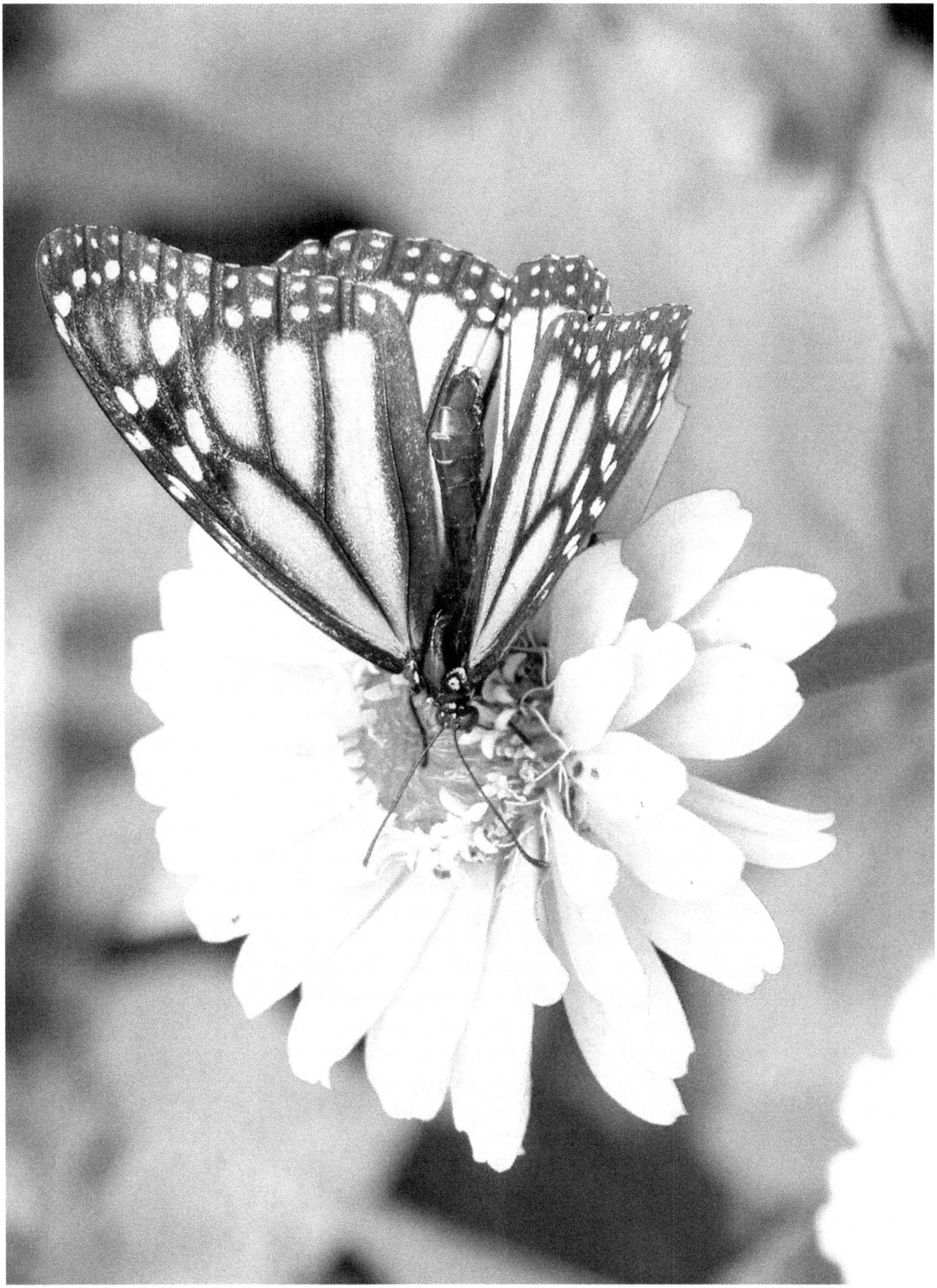

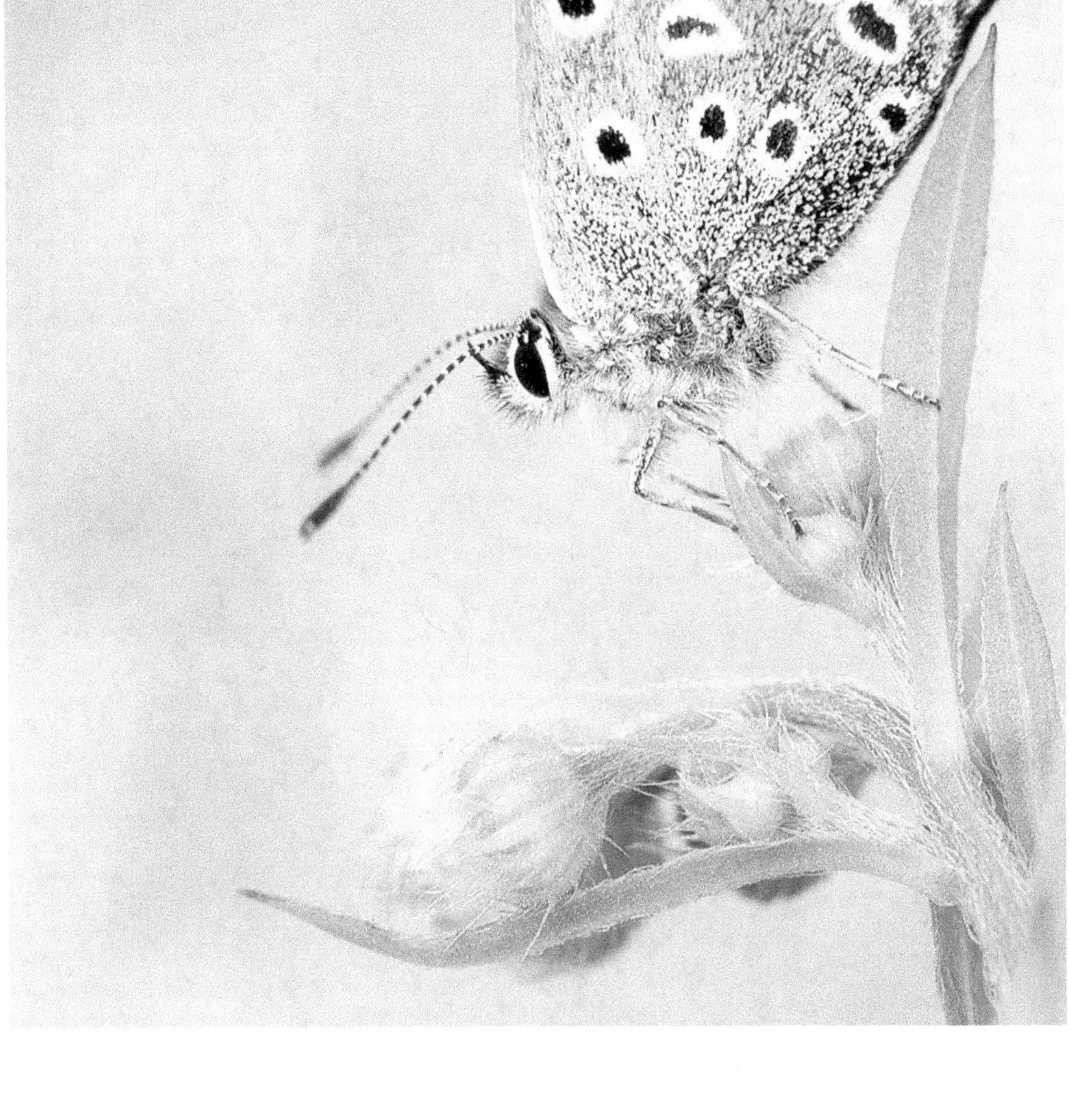

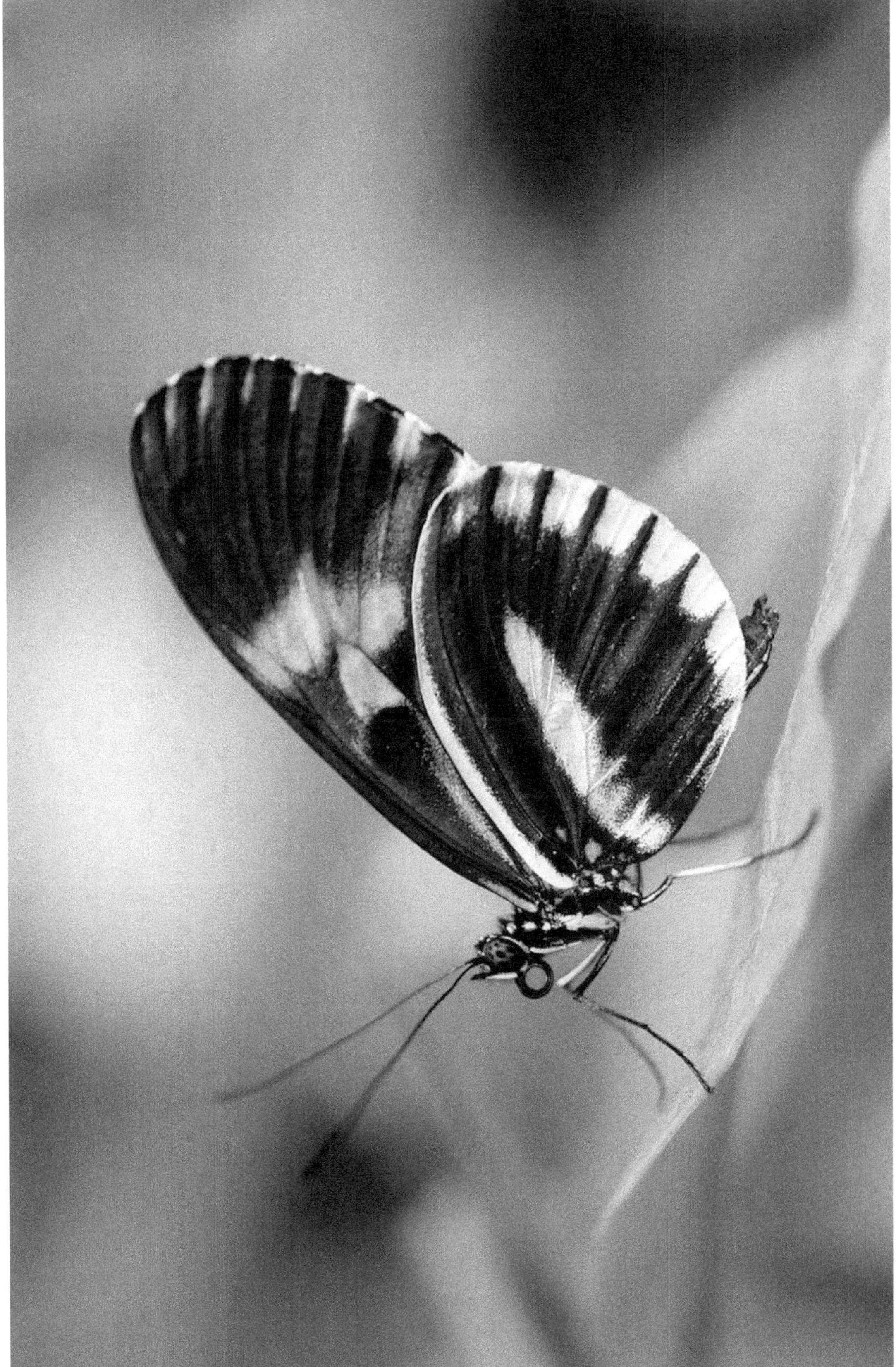

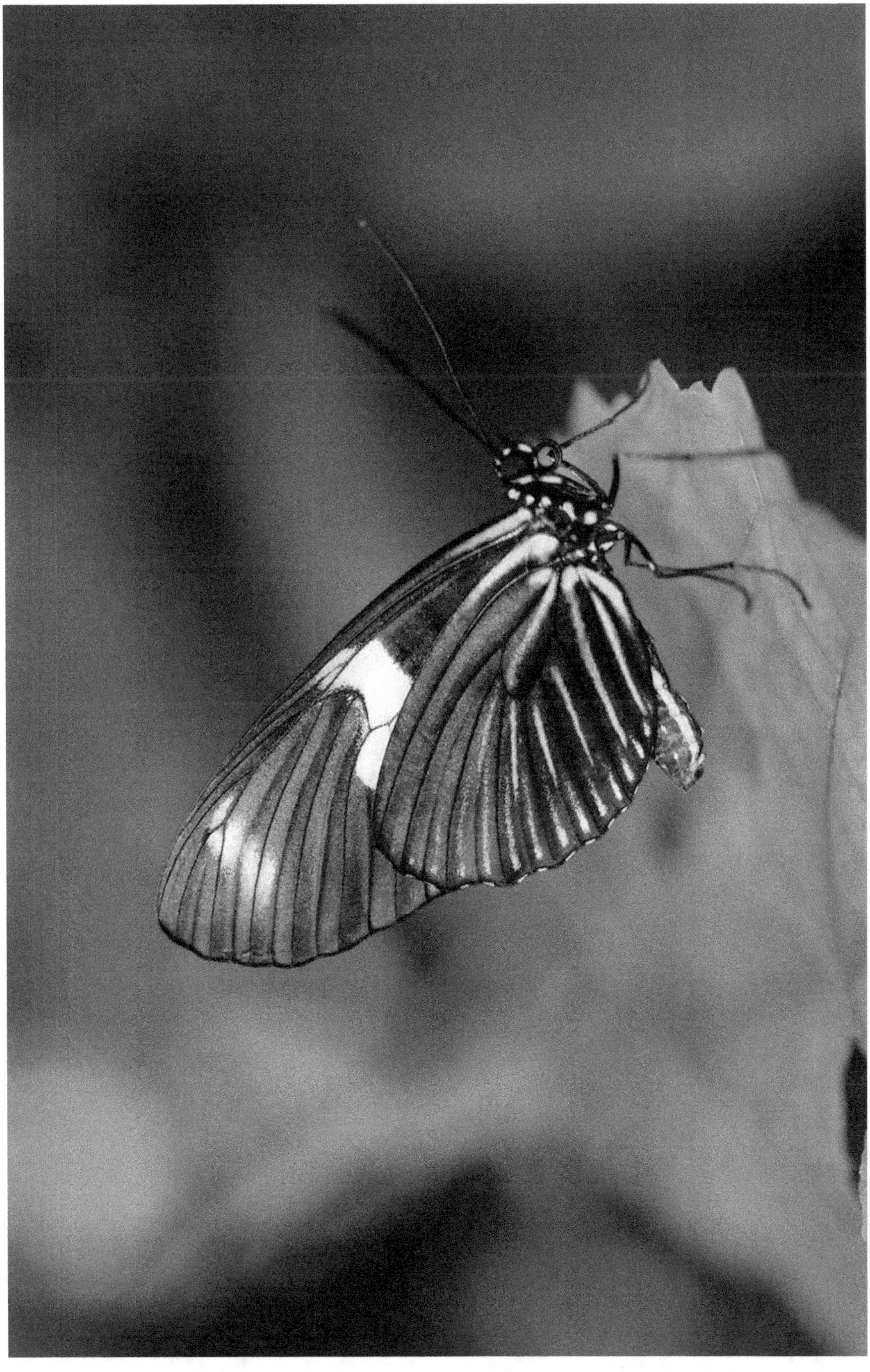

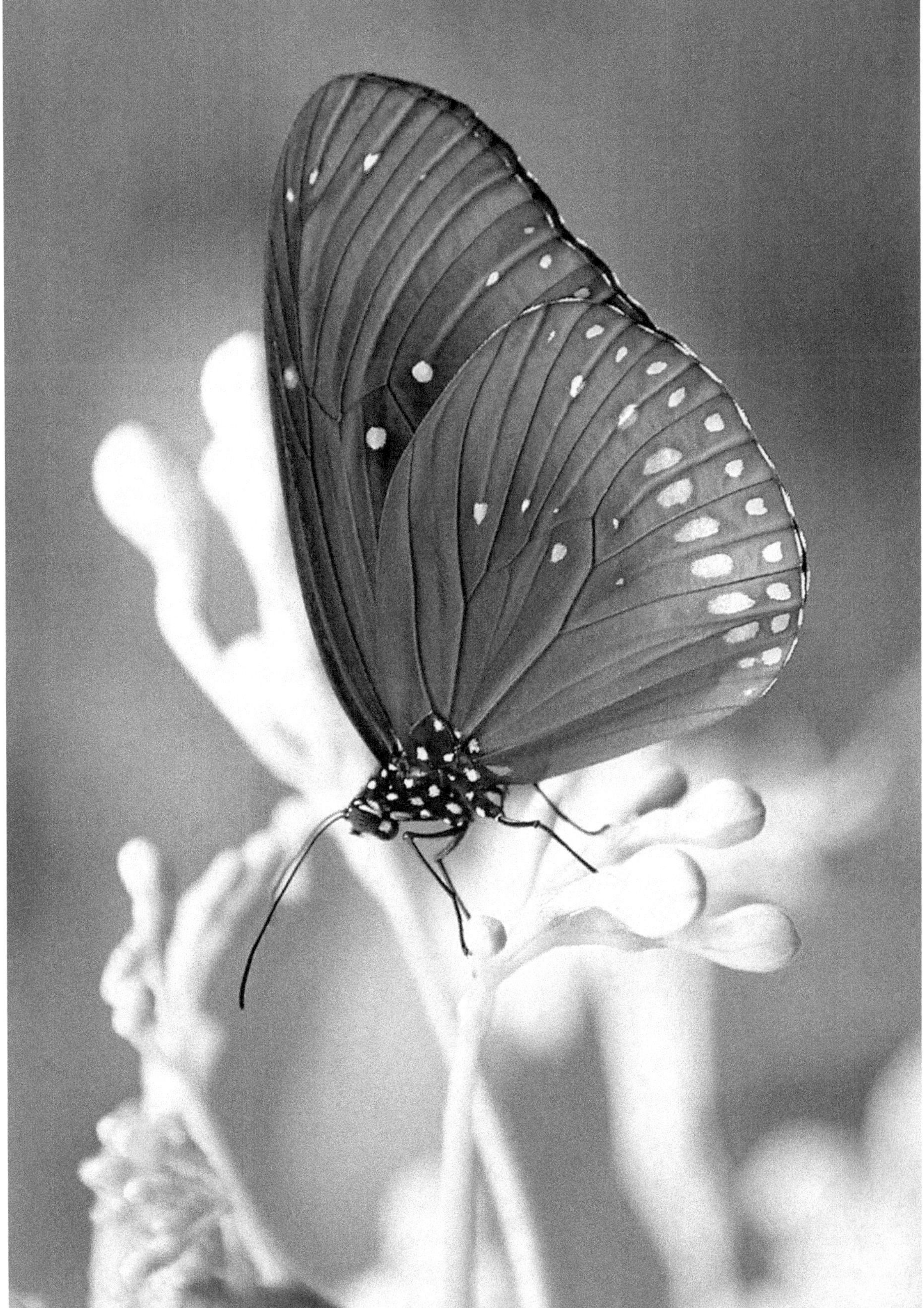

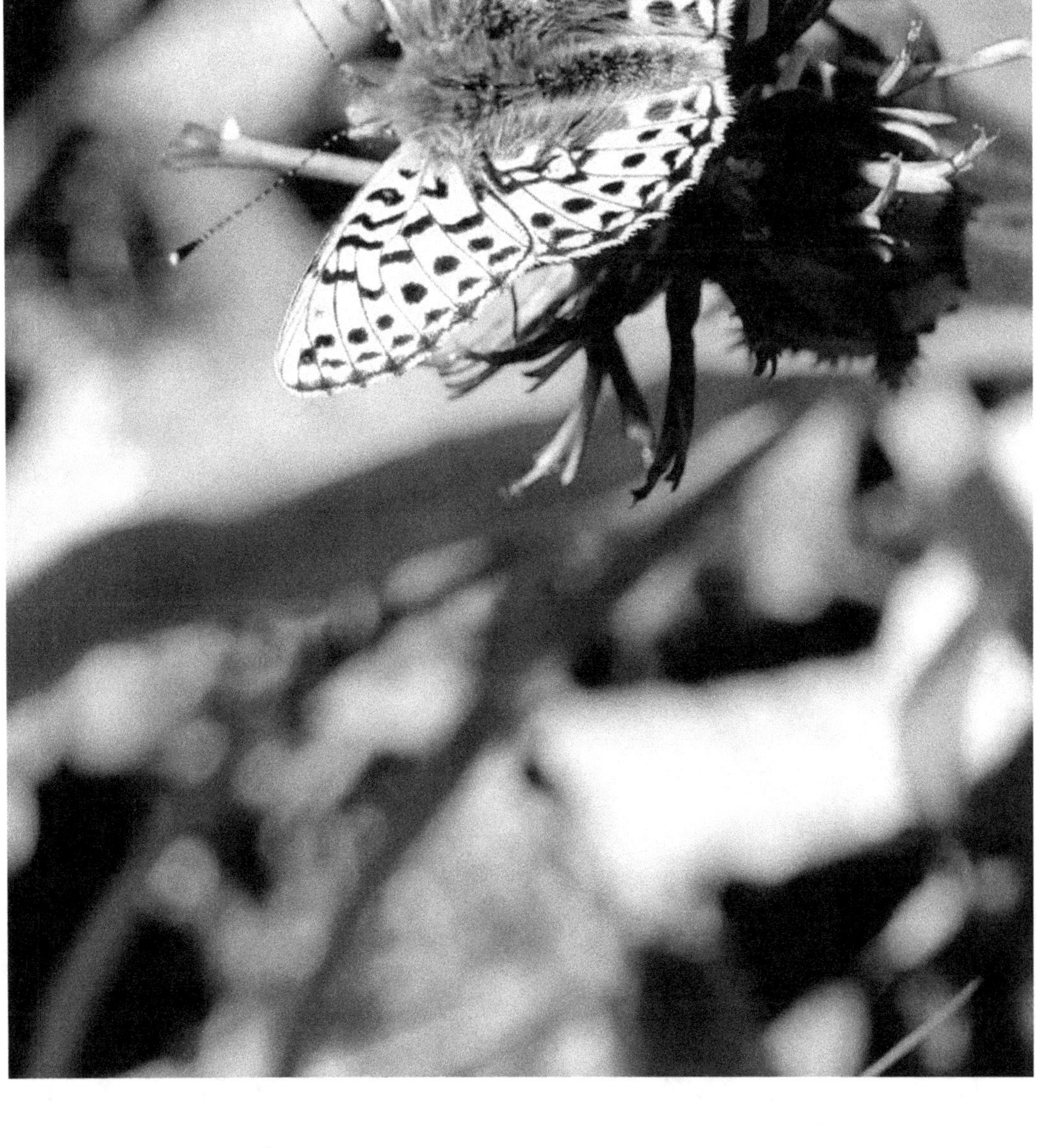

www.ingramcontent.com/pod-product-compliance
Lightning Source LLC
Chambersburg PA
CBHW052015280526
45793CB00005B/991
* 9 7 8 1 5 3 5 3 0 1 8 6 2 *